The Ultin Drummer Joke Book

Mikey Chlanda

Q. What did the drummer get on his IQ test?

A. Drool.

Q. How can you tell that there's a drummer knocking on your door?

A. When you tell him to come in, he's two beats late.

Q. Why does the drummer keep knocking on your door?

A. Drummers never know when to come in.

Q. Why do bands have drummers?

A. Everybody needs an asshole.

Q. How many drummers does it take to screw in a light bulb?

A. 101. One to screw it in, the other hundred to say "That's not the way Neil Peart would have done it."

Second answer – None. Hell, they don't even realize it's dark in the room yet.

Third answer – None. They don't screw anything that doesn't move. Unless they're really drunk – then anything goes.

Q. Did you hear about the drummer that went to Harvard?

A. Neither did I.

Q. What's the difference between a drummer and a homeless guy?

A. The homeless guy will eventually get his shit together.

Q. What do you call a drummer's girlfriend?

A. A prostitute.

Q. What's the difference between a drummer and a puppy?

Eventually the puppy grows up and stops whining.

Q. What's the difference between a drummer and a government savings bond?

A. The savings bond eventually matures and makes money.

Q. Why are drummers always losing their watches?

A. Hey, if they could keep time, they wouldn't be drummers.

Q. Why does a drummer's girlfriend always have to be on top when they screw?

A. Because drummers only know how to fuck up.

Q. What's the difference between a drummer and an extra-large pizza?

A. The pizza can feed a family of four.

Q. What does a drummer use for birth control?

A. His personality. And if that doesn't work, he uses the rhythm method.

Q. How can you tell if a drum kit is level?

A. Drool comes out of both sides of the drummer's mouth.

Q. What do you call someone who hangs out with musicians?

A. A drummer.

Q. How do you get a drummer off your front porch?

A. Pay him for the pizza.

How can you tell when a drummer is on your front porch?

A. The knocking speeds up...it slows down...it speeds up.

Q. What do you call a drummer who just broke up with his girlfriend?

A. Homeless.

Q. What's the last thing a drummer says before his band breaks up?

A. "Hey guys, I just wrote some songs we should try out."

Q. What does a stripper do with her asshole right before she goes on stage?

A. She drops him off at band practice with his drum kit.

A guy flies down to one of the islands. As he gets off the plane, he hears ominous drumming in the background. "What's that drumming about?"

The stewardess just shakes her head and replies, "When drumming stops, very bad."

As he flags down a taxi, he asks the driver the same thing as they're putting his bags in the cab. The driver has the same response – a shake of the head and "When drumming stops, very bad."

He gets to the hotel and the bellhop is helping with the guy's luggage. The drumming is still going on. "What's with the drumming?"

"Oh mister, when drumming stops, very bad."

"I get that. Everyone's telling me that. But what happens when the drumming stops?"

The bellhop just shakes his head and looks sad. "Bass solo starts."

Q. What does Ginger Baker have in common with coffee?

A. Both suck without Cream.

The missionary looked up from dinner, worried about the ominous drumming that had been going on in the background for hours. He mentioned to the chief, "I don't like the sound of those drums."

The chief replied, "Neither do I, but our regular drummer is in jail."

===

Did you hear about the drummer that was so bad, even the other drummers noticed?

Q. What do you call a group of drummers?

A. A drunk tank.

Q. How does a drummer know it's closing time at the bar?

A. All the beer's gone.

Q. What do you call a drummer with half a brain?

A. Gifted.

Q. What do you call a drummer's wife?

A. Deaf, dumb, and blind

Q. What do you call a drummer's girlfriend that stays with him for five years?

A. Saint Teresa

Two drummers go to India. Across the market square one day, they see an elderly lady. One drummer says, "Hey, I think that's Mother Teresa."

The other drummer says, "Ahhh, you're full of it. I bet you a dollar she's not.

The first one says "You're on" and goes over to ask the woman if she is, really in fact, Mother Teresa.
The old woman turns around and snarls at him. "Fuck you, you goddamn pervert. Get the fuck away from me before I call the goddamn police." She stalks off before he can say a word.

Dejected, the drummer walks back to his buddy. "Man, now we'll never know."

Q. How can you tell that the drummer really sucks?

A. Even the bass player notices.

Q. What does a sneeze have in common with a drum solo?

A. You can feel one coming on, but there's not a damn thing you can do about it.

Q. Why does the drummer leave his sticks on the dashboard of his car?

A. So he can park in the handicapped spaces at the mall.

Q. How many drummers does it take to screw in a lightbulb?

A. None, because they think you push it in.

Q. What are a drummer's first intelligent words?

A. "You want fries with that?"

Three drummers walk into a bar. Which is pretty funny when you think about it, because you'd assume the others would have noticed how much it hurt the first drummer.

Q. Why does the drummer walk his third-grader to school?

A. Well, why not? He's in fifth.

Q. How many drummers does it take to change a lightbulb?

A. Just one, but only after being told very slowly and in small words why it needs to be done.

Q. How many drummers does it take to screw in a lightbulb?

A. Just one, as long as you tell him the stripper inside of it puts out.

Q. How can you tell if a drummer is well-hung?

A. You can't slide your finger in between the noose and his neck.

Q. How many drummers does it take to change a lightbulb?

A. None. They have drum machines for that now.

Q. How can you tell if a drummer did the crossword puzzle?

A. All the blank squares have been colored in.

Q. How do you get a drummer to stop biting his nails?

A. Tell him to put on his shoes

Q. How do you get a drummer out of a tree?

A. Cut the rope.

Q. How do you get a hippo out of quicksand?

A. Toss a drummer in there with it. The hippo will find a way out

Q. How can you make a drummer's car more streamlined?

A. Take the Domino's Pizza sign off of it

Q. How does a drummer know which way to put on his underwear?

A. Yellow in front, brown in back...

Q. How many drummers can you fit in a phone booth?

A. None. How is he supposed to fit his drum kit in there?

Q. How many drummers does it take to wallpaper a room?

A. Depends on how thin you slice them

"Mom, when I grow up, I want to be a drummer."
His mother just looked at him and said, "I've told you before, Johnny, you have to make up your mind which one you want to be."

So a drummer walks into a bar... man did that look like it hurt!

Q. What do you call a drummer with a credit card?

A. Married

Q. What do you call it when a bunch of musicians are doing shots at the bar?

A. Drum solo.

Q. What do you call a guy who hangs out with musicians?

A. A drummer

Q. Why is it sadder to see a possum run over in the road than a drummer run over in the road?

A. The possum might have been on the way to a gig

Q. What do you do if you find a drum kit in the dumpster?

A. Leave it there.

Q. What do you call a drummer in a three-piece suit?

Defendant

Q. What does it mean when a drummer is in your bed gasping for breath and calling your name?

A. You didn't hold the pillow down long enough.

Q. What is the definition of perfect pitch?

A. When the drum kit lands on top of the accordion without hitting the side walls of the dumpster

Q. What's the difference between a dead possum and a dead drummer?

A. There's two sets of tire tracks on the drummer, one forward, and one going back just to make sure.

Q. What is the difference between an onion and a drummer?

A. Nobody cries when you chop up a drummer.

Q. What's the difference between a drummer and a vacuum cleaner?

A. You don't have to plug in a drummer for him to suck.

Q. What is the dynamic range of a drum kit?

A. On and off

Q. What's the ultimate sincere compliment you can pay a drummer?

A. "Nice tooth."

Q. What should you call a drummer?

A. It doesn't matter. They won't listen anyway

Q. What's the best protection the Secret Service could have against a Presidential assassination?

A. Make a drummer the Vice-President.

Q. What's the best thing to play on a drum set?

A. Solitaire

Q. What's the biggest lie told to a drummer?

A. "Hang on a sec and I'll help you with your gear."

Q. What's the definition of a gentleman?

A. A gentleman knows how to play the drums but doesn't.

Q. What's the definition of "relative minor"?

A. She's the drummer's girlfriend

Q. What's the difference between a bass drum and a snare drum?

A. The bass drum gives off more heat and burns longer.

Q. What's the difference between a drummer and garbage?

A. The garbage gets taken out at least once a week.

Q. What's the difference between a drummer and a drum machine?

A. You only have to punch the information into a drum machine once.

Q. What's the difference between a drum set and a chainsaw?

A. You can tune a chainsaw as well as pawn it

Q. What's the difference between a drum set and a trampoline?

A. You take your shoes off when you jump on a trampoline.

Q. Why are all the drummers moving to LA?

A. It's the only city that they can spell

Q. What's the ideal weight for a drummer?

A. Four and a half pounds including the urn.

Q. What does a vacuum cleaner have in common with a drum kit?

A. They both have a half-full dirt bag sitting behind them.

Q. Why is a the steering wheel in a drummer's car so small?

A. So he can drive with handcuffs on.

Q. Why do horses have one more brain cell than drummers?

So when the horses march in a parade, they can avoid the horseshit on the road.

Q. Why is a drum machine better than a drummer?

A. It can actually keep time and it won't sleep with your girlfriend.

Q. What's the difference between a drum machine and a drummer?

A. The drum machine has a cute chick on each arm

Two drums and a cymbal fall down the stairs. Ba boom boom boom peesh.

Printed in Great Britain
by Amazon

19648633R00020